Hip, Hippo, HOORAY for
FIONA!

A PHOTOGRAPHIC BIOGRAPHY

by JAN SHERBIN
with photos from the CINCINNATI ZOO

To Fiona,

who brought happiness
into a troubled world.

Photographs from the Cincinnati Zoo and Botanical
Garden.

Book design by Chuck Rekow.

Text set in Nolan Next.

ISBN 978-0-692-94935-1

Library of Congress Control Number: 2017914185

This book is made in the United States of America.

Exciting news at the Cincinnati Zoo!
A baby hippo is on the way. Bibi's going to be a mother in spring. Hooray!

But one winter day, Bibi moves through the water in strange patterns.
Something is happening.

Oh, no! She's having the baby NOW!
It's way too early.

Bibi waddles out of her pool. A glistening brown hippo baby slides out of her.
Bibi looks.
She sniffs.
She lies down.

She can't help her baby.

Is the baby alive?
Her eyes are open.
She's breathing!

She is the smallest live hippo anyone has ever seen. **Very, very,** very much smaller than any other hippo babies.

Is she ready to live outside her mother?
No.

Does she have a chance?
Maybe. But she'll need help.

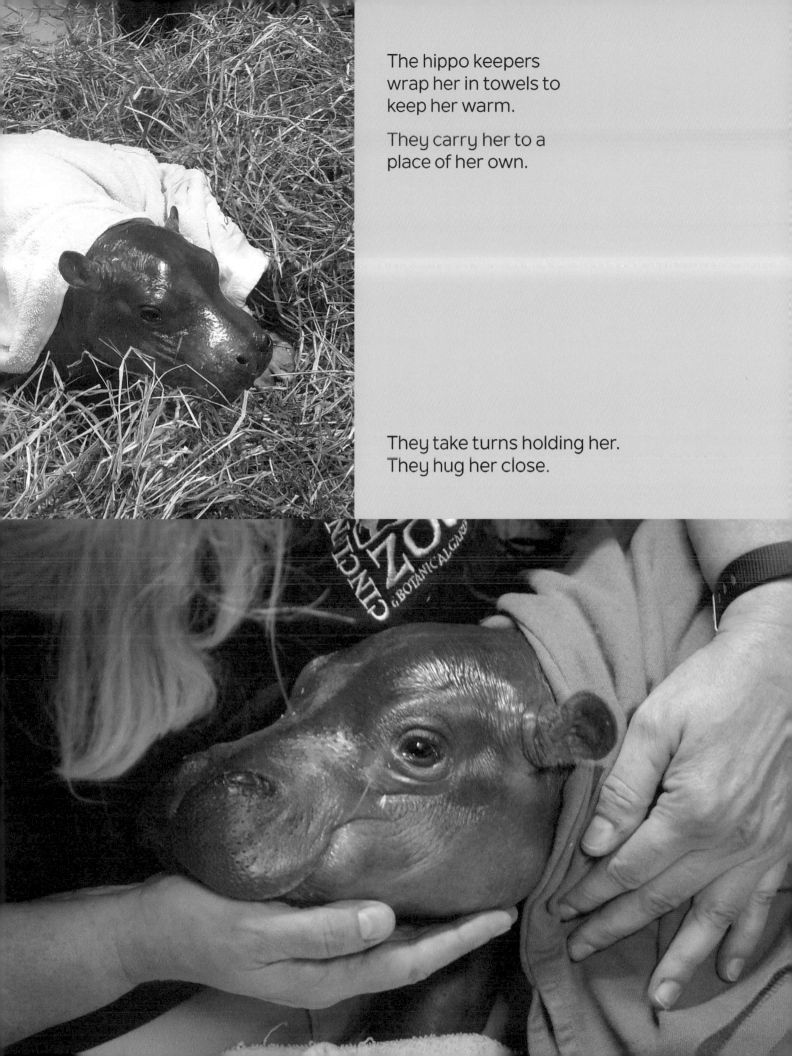

The hippo keepers wrap her in towels to keep her warm.

They carry her to a place of her own.

They take turns holding her. They hug her close.

The tiny hippo has trouble breathing. They put a tube into her nose when she sleeps so she can breathe better.

She must stay wet.
But she can't hold her breath to go underwater. The keepers place her in a baby pool.

She needs to eat. Her mother is the only place she can get the right kind of milk. But she isn't strong enough to stand under Bibi to nurse.

The keepers have a crazy idea: They will milk Bibi like a farmer milks a cow. No one has ever milked a hippo, but they will try *anything* to keep the newborn alive!

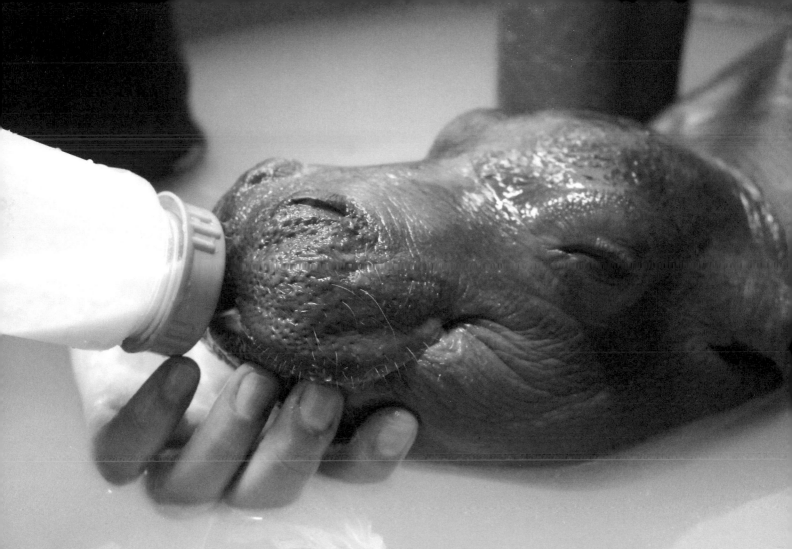

They put Bibi's milk in a bottle.

The baby can drink from the bottle if someone holds up her chin.

Come on, little hippo! Drink!

She drinks.
She becomes stronger.
She takes her first wobbly steps.

Go, little hippo! Go!

The keepers fall in love with the tiny hippo. They sit with her in a little plastic swimming pool.

Millions of people meet the baby hippo on the Internet. They fall in love with her, too.

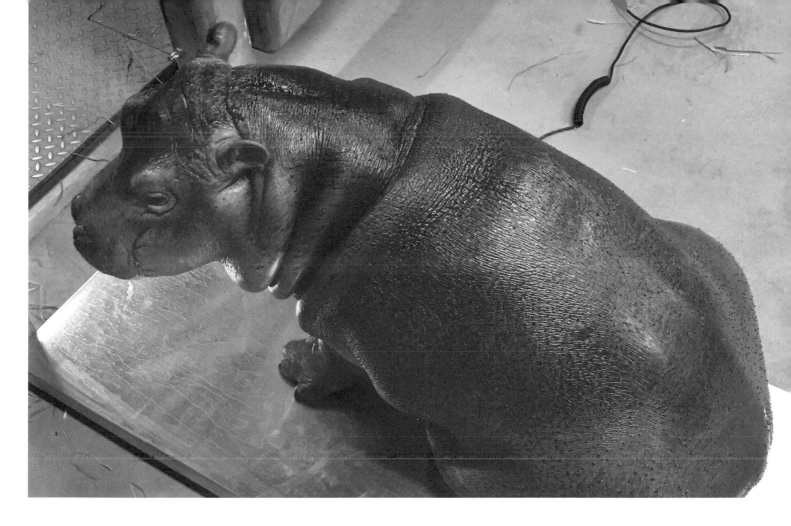

The little hippo wants more milk than her mother can give. The zoo figures out how to make her a baby formula. Now she has plenty of milk.

Every day, the little hippo sits on a scale. She's getting heavier! But she needs to get a *lot* heavier to weigh as much as the smallest hippo baby ever known.

Her keepers think she might be able to do that. *If* things go well.

Fight, little hippo! Fight!

Her keepers think she'll fight harder if she has a name.
They call her

FIONA

Come on, little Fiona! Grow strong and healthy!

Fiona fights hard, but things *don't* go well.

Little hippo teeth break through her gums. Her mouth hurts. She won't drink from her bottle.

She loses weight. She loses energy.

Her keepers rub her gums with cold cloths. They give her toys to chew.

Still, Fiona doesn't drink.

Things are going very badly.

Then things get even worse:

Fiona's insides are drying out. This is an emergency.

Animal doctors want to send fluids into Fiona. They think they can do this with needles stuck into the tiny veins in her leg. But every time they try, Fiona's veins break. She gets sicker and sicker.

Time for another idea:

The keepers call the hospital that cares for human babies born too soon. Nurses there rush over to help Fiona.

They bring needles and tubes that fit into the tiniest human babies. They bring an ultrasound machine that can find stronger veins deep inside Fiona's leg.

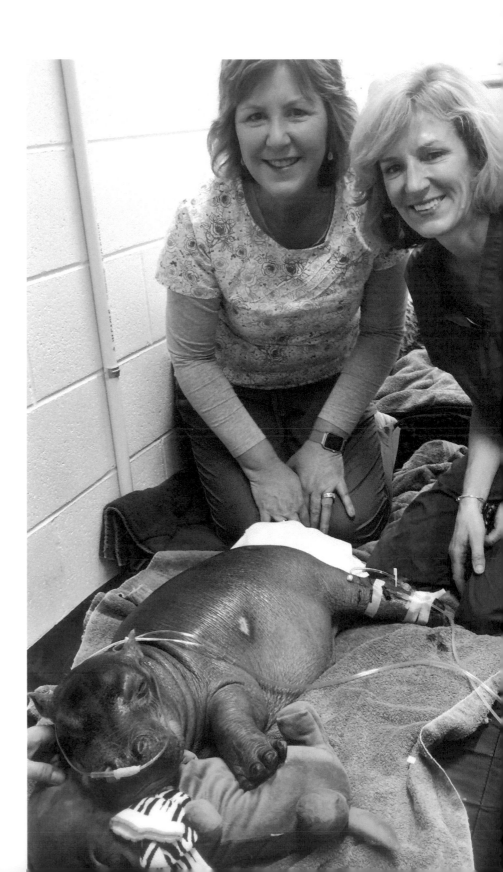

For two days and two nights, her keepers watch closely, every minute. They make sure the needles and tubes do their job.

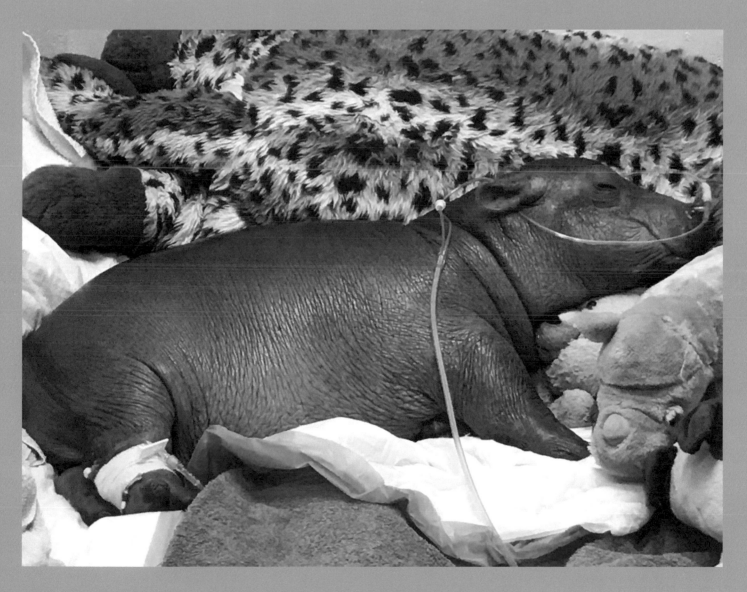

Come on, Fiona! Don't give up, Fiona!

Finally, Fiona's mouth feels better.

Grunt!

That means she's hungry. She drinks her bottle again.

Fiona gets a little **bigger**,

then a little **bigger than that.**

She grows to **twice her size** when she was born.

She needs a bigger bottle!

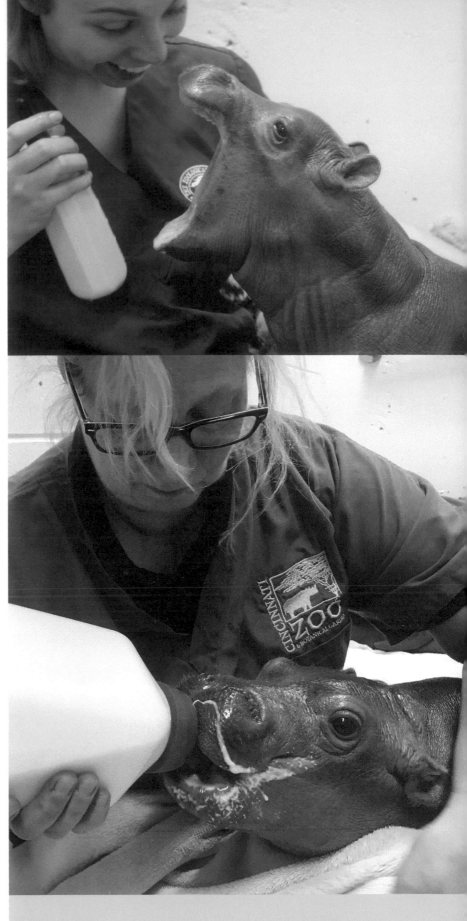

Slurp, Slurp . . . BURP!

She needs a bigger swimming pool!

She still snuggles with her keepers.

In spring, about the time Fiona was supposed to be born, her keepers turn on a hose. Will Fiona stand under the water and catch it in her mouth?

That's what hippos do.

Fiona opens her mouth wide.

She catches the water!

That's when her keepers know it's time for Fiona to learn to become a big hippo.

Fiona isn't sure she likes this idea.

Fiona's pool is small. She can sit on the bottom and keep her nose above water.

It's easy.

Sorry, Fiona.
This is not what big hippos do.

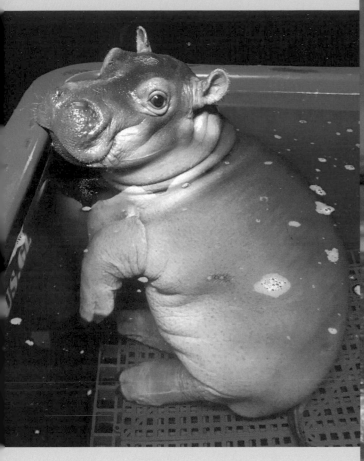

Fiona must go into water above her head.
This is what big hippos do.

Fiona practices holding her breath under water.
Good job, Fiona!

Fiona is ready to go into deeper water. Her keepers put her in a
bigger pool. They fill it higher and higher every day.

Dive! Push!

Fiona dives. She pushes her feet onto the bottom to come back up.
Isn't this fun, Fiona?

In her room, Fiona smells other hippos. What a wonderful stink!

She hears them. They **SNORT!**
It sounds like they have something stuck in their throats.

They **bellow** loudly. This sounds like rumbling thunder.

Snort! Bellow! Fiona makes hippo noises, too,
in her little Fiona way.

snort!

bellow!

Who are the other hippos?
They are Fiona's mother, Bibi, and her father, Henry.

They are **HUGE.**

They are a *hundred* times **BIGGER** than Fiona.

Will they scare her?

YES!

Fiona meets her mother.
Fiona runs away.

Be brave, Fiona!
Be brave!

Fiona becomes brave *and* curious. She touches noses with Bibi through a fence.

Does Fiona know Bibi is her mother?

Does Bibi know Fiona is her baby?

The keepers take away the fence. Bibi lies still while Fiona licks her. Then Bibi opens her mouth, showing her big hippo teeth.

Run, Fiona! **RUN!**

Fiona does not run. She puts her whole head into Bibi's mouth.
She understands Bibi is inviting her to explore.
This is how hippos make friends.

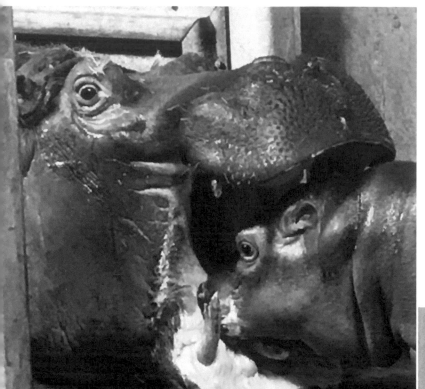

Now it is time for Fiona to meet her father, Henry.
Henry is even bigger than Bibi.
Fiona meets him through the fence.

He licks her.

Then he swings his head. This means he wants to be left alone.
Fiona waits quietly. She doesn't pester him.

Fiona admires the way Henry opens his mouth very **WIDE**

Fiona practices doing that.

Fiona grows tall enough to peek out a small window in her room.

She smells the fresh spring air.

Her keepers want her to go outdoors.

But it's fun to stay in her room with her keepers and her toys.

Why can't she stay inside?

Because, Fiona,
you need to be a hippo.

Here's a push.

The keepers take Fiona outdoors to the big pool. They know what to do. They go with her into the water.

You did it, Fiona! You're outdoors! You're in the big pool!

A waterfall!
Fiona catches water in her mouth.

Sand!
It feels so good on a wet hippo.

One day, Fiona goes to the big pool.
Bibi is there.

Fiona is afraid to go in with Bibi.

Bibi knows what to do.
She stays by Fiona's side.

Fiona feels more comfortable.
She goes into the pool.

Bibi tries to keep her in
shallow water.

Instead, Fiona takes off into the
deep part of the pool.

How brave you are, Fiona!

Indoors, Henry still won't play with Fiona.

The keepers have an idea:
Maybe Henry will play in a group of three. He comes to the outdoor pool when Fiona and Bibi are in it.

Fiona invites him to play.

Henry doesn't know how to play with a baby hippo. Sometimes he plays a little roughly. Bibi shoos him away.

Fiona asks for more lessons on opening her mouth wIDE.

Fiona nibbles her parents.

At nap time, they snooze in a huddle. It's hard to tell who is who.
Finally, they are together as a cozy, happy family.

Fiona needs to do one more thing.

She needs to meet the people who come to the zoo.

They will shout and squeal. They will jump up and down. They will bang on the glass. They will flash bright lights when they take photos.

Will they scare Fiona? They might.

Fiona's keepers have a plan:

They pretend to be zoo visitors. They hope this will help Fiona feel comfortable when she meets her fans.

The big day comes!

Fiona trots to the outdoor pool and finds strangers greeting her.

She is not afraid.

She puts her face up to the glass to say hello.

She poses for photos.

Fiona is a hippo **STAR!**

Hip, hippo, HOORAY for

FIONA!

ABOUT FIONA

Fiona was born on January 24, 2017. She weighed only twenty-nine pounds.

Before Fiona, the smallest newborn Nile hippo known to survive weighed fifty-five pounds. A newborn hippo can weigh up to one hundred twenty pounds.

On the day Fiona drank from the hose, she weighed about ninety pounds.

When Fiona is three years old:

- She will weigh as much as a car.
- She will spend sixteen hours a day in water.
- She will be able to stay under water for five minutes.
- She will be able to run faster than a person.

It looks like Fiona is swimming, but she isn't. Like all hippos, she runs along the bottom of her pool. When she wants air, she pushes off with her feet to pop up to the surface.

Or she can push off and drift in the water.

Or roll onto her back.

Or even do somersaults!

Fiona keeps her eyes open under water.

She likes to eat hay, watermelon, apples, and lettuce.

Bibi treats Fiona gently and with patience. We will never know whether Bibi and Fiona realize they are mother and daughter.

Team Fiona: Cincinnati Zoo and Cincinnati Children's Hospital staff who worked hard to pull off a hippo-size miracle.

THANKS TO . . .

The Cincinnati Zoo & Botanical Garden, especially Chad Yelton, Michelle Curley, Amy LaBarbara, Christina Gorsuch, Jenna Wingate.

My writer colleagues who helped me tell Fiona's **BIG** story in a *little* way so the youngest children can take part in it.

Chuck Rekow, who designed text and photos into a beautiful keepsake book.

Photo Credits:

Michelle Curley, Angela Hatke, David Jenike, Dan Turoczi, Jenna Wingate, Mark Dumont, Kathy Newton, DJJAM Photo, Dana Burke, Lisa Hubbard, Tami Ware, Christina Gorsuch, Teresa Truesdale.

This book was made in the United States of America
in cooperation with the Cincinnati Zoo.

CincinnatiZoo.org

CPSIA information can be obtained at www.ICGtesting.com
Printed in the USA
LVIW01n1358191217
560252LV00002B/2